1 MONTH OF
FREE
READING

at
www.ForgottenBooks.com

By purchasing this book you are eligible for one month membership to ForgottenBooks.com, giving you unlimited access to our entire collection of over 1,000,000 titles via our web site and mobile apps.

To claim your free month visit:

www.forgottenbooks.com/free149103

ISBN 978-0-483-60963-1
PIBN 10149103

THE MONARCH

AND OTHER POEMS

BY

JOHN H. FLAGG

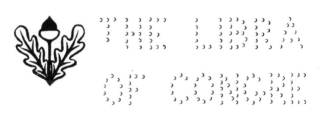

PRIVATELY PRINTED

NEW YORK

Published December, 1902

Printed by
CARROLL J. POST, Jr.
New York

To Edward Quintard, whose skillful
service as a physician and unfailing devotion
as a friend have made me a double debtor,
I inscribe these pages in lasting gratitude.

J. H. F.

POEMS

THE MONARCH.

EHOLD!—The Monarch, Time, am I,
   Whom none shall balk nor dare deny!
   I will supreme in every clime
Where man would make my deeds a crime,
And thrones that rule mankind through awe,
   To me decree no binding law!
Before a mortal crown was worn
   Or pompous king or queen was born
My sceptre swung from every throne —
   My mandates rang from zone to zone.

My mission here is to despoil —
  To do it well, my only toil; —
Man's ceaseless sob and pleading prayer
  To my dull ear no wailings bear.
I work alone, and have no friend
  To praise, encourage or commend.
With muffled feet I stride ahead
  And make no sound where'er I tread.
As youth and health to me belong,
  I need no rest to keep me strong,
And weary not by day nor year
  In loading death upon my bier,
Nor reaching down into the grave
  To turn to dust what Nature gave.

Behold my work already done
  With yet my purpose scarce begun! —
Where tropic suns now smite the earth
  Gleamed icebergs once, of ponderous girth;

Where ocean billows once leapt high
   Now Chimborazo cleaves the sky;
Where primal Rome was hewn and reared
   Five Romes in turn have disappeared;
Where Karnak raised her mighty walls
   The sluggish reptile creeps and crawls;
Where Charthage stood and held her sway
   Wild forest beasts pursue their prey.

The lord of skies and seas and lands,
   I spare no work of human hands!—
The sculptured forms by genius wrought;
   The monuments where heroes fought;
The chiselled altars hewn from stone;
   The palaces where kings are grown;
Earth's navies on the salted seas;
   The mitred pope on bended knees;
The fanes upreared by pious hands;
   The pyramids on Egypt's sands;

Man's castles and his rustic homes;

His temples with their gilded domes;

His campaniles and his towers

Where tolls the knell of passing hours;

His treasures, trophies, battle-won;

His states and empires scarce begun—

Alike shall perish with the rest

And turn to dust at my behest!

Yet mark besides what is to be

And naught can frustrate my decree!—

Proud Aetna's flames shall cease to burn

And glaciers melt and freeze in turn;

To nebulae I'll change the earth

And pay back Nature's debt with dearth:—

I'll pluck the planets from the skies

(Which dazzle now man's wondering eyes)

And then blot out the blazing sun

And turn to vapor whence begun:—

Then, midst the waste, behold my throne—

A Monarch still, though left alone!

THE BROOK.

———

I AM the brook, the nimble brook,
  Born in my tranquil, shaded nook
  Mid solemn hills and mountain peak
Where nature every language speaks.

Unlike the footed beasts of earth —
  So frail and helpless at their birth —
I straightway creep, then stride, then run,
  To greet my first uprising sun.

On, on I rush with quickened pace
    And force my way from place to place,
While lesser brooklets eager flow
    To swell my volume as 1 go.

The alders nod when I pass by;
    The reeds and rushes courtesy;
And where the lilies rise and float
    I suck rare nectar from each throat.

When I grow weary or depressed
    I loiter at my pools to rest,
Then hurry on with doubled haste
    To catch the hours allowed to waste.

When lo, I'm throttled as I wend
  And harnessed like a beast to lend
My help to man's dependent hand
  Which halts me with its rude command.

Thus forced, I tread man's endless wheel;
  I grind his grist and mould his steel;
His looms I work with faithful hand,
  And all his varied arts expand.

But soon I break from this embrace
  And hasten from the servile place,
But grieve to find I've grown ten fold
  Since down the mountain-side I bowled.

At length I wake, as from a dream,
  To find myself a tidal stream
That brings rank sea-salt to my tongue,
  A taste unknown when I was young.

And now I hear the ocean roar
  And tremble at my fate in store;
I scent his breath and quail with awe,
  But helpless, yield to Nature's law;—

To Nature's law I bow content,
  That law which none can circumvent;
The hand that lifts the oceans' tide
  Will reach to me and then abide!

RUE to each trust and best when trusted mo

For Country first, though facing peace or w

Making, in peace, its greatness greater st

While yet in war his young but manly breast

On many a blood-soaked, death-strewn battle-field

Was bared to shield a Nation's heart from harm.

This man of God, born fit to lead the way

And lift mankind to nobler, loftier heights,

Alas! by Anarch's poisoned fang lies slain!

And when he fell, lo, in remotest lands

Were mingled tears and solemn, tolling bells

Proclaiming anguish equal to our own.

That blameless life, — that apt, sagacious tongue

Though hushed on earth forevermore, yet speak

As with an angel's trumpet and declare

The better life is lingering with us still.

September, 1901.

ON A DEW DROP.

HAT is that chaste, that spark-
    ling thing,
    Which to the rose at dawn
doth cling,
And nestled near its throbbing breast
Plays ardent lover while a guest?

'Tis but a tear of weeping night —
    The weeping of a glad delight —
Till startled by obtruding day
    Night, fearing capture, steals away.

CHILDHOOD'S HOME.

DREAMED of busy childhood days,
   where sunshine ever clung,
Back in my country home again
   when this old heart was young;
Through one brief hour of ecstacy, when every
   thought was bliss,
With manhood's cares forsaken, what spell could
   be like this?

My ravished eyes sought every place—each
object they once knew —
With nothing changed in all these years and
nothing added new;
Transfixed I stood amid the scenes so long ob-
scured from sight,
As through the windows shone, I thought, a
consecrated light.

I saw the row of flower-pots upon the window-
sill,
Wherein grew sweet geraniums that drooped
with thirst until
At sunset mother sprinkled them, and fondled
each with care:—
Methought, to gladden my return, their frag-
rance was still there.

I saw the old melodeon whose notes I'd
    often heard

Commingled with my mother's voice that hal-
    lowed every word;

This, long since, joined the choir unseen in an-
    thems sung on high:—

I sometimes think I hear it now through cloud-
    rifts in the sky.

In yonder nook—its 'customed place—stood
    father's old oak chair—

Descended from ancestral lines—a gift from heir
    to heir;—

As if to stay each stranger hand and shield it from
    all harm,

A spider here had spun her web outstretched from
    arm to arm.

How often here I'd clambered to my father's
    waiting knee,
To hear his thrilling stories told ofi deeds on land
    and sea,—
Ofi Indian scalpers on the plains,—of pirates fierce
    and bold,—
Of hunters' daring for wild beasts—and others
    search for gold.

Here was the book-case just as when, at pleasant
    evening time,
I searched the well-worn volumes through for
    picture or for rhyme:
For just plain books I did not care,—they baffled
    me with lore—
Whatever one I tried to read I soon declared a
    bore.

There hung the old gilt mirror still, near to the
    parlor door,
Where I'd intently gazed upon my new clothes
    from the store,
And once had donned my brother's suit when to
    the glass I ran,
To see how big and brave I'd look when I be-
    came a man.

There stood the same old kitchen stove, where
    many a nipping day,
I'd held my freezing, outstretched hands when I
    came in from play;
This good old friend had one grave fault—it
    burned out wood so fast—
I lugged it in incessantly, until the cold months
    passed.

Its glowing sides my mother sought in patient
willing toil,
To make the good things for us all that careless
cooks might spoil;
She always baked me special pies and cookies,
cakes, galore,
And yet I claimed I grew so fast I needed
just one more.

There peered the old remorseless clock that
watched me argus-eyed,
And when my bed-time hour arrived my
patience oft had tried;
'Twas then I claimed it ran too fast, while
mother claimed 'twas slow;—
Whatever my contention was I always had to
go—

Go to my far-off attic bed when mother led
the way,
Whose candle and assuring words my fears did
not allay;—
She bore away the candle, after kissing me
good-night,
But all through life I've felt that kiss and seen
that vanished light.

There was the same old ample shelf that father
called his own,
Where he kept Bible, pipe and pen and all
odd things were thrown;
Beneath it, hung the almanac, that said in
letters bold,
"*About this time look out for squalls*" — which
prophecy controlled.

I heard the rattling Autumn hail upon the
window-pane,
Forewarning that dread Winter days were steal-
ing back again;
Thanksgiving was approaching, too,—that boon
from old Cape Cod,—
Ordained by pious Pilgrim sires, in gratefulness
to God.

I whistled then for dear "old Jack," who hasten-
ed to my side,—
That noble, true, confiding friend—my comrade
and my pride;
Where'er I strayed he too must go,—I always
felt his touch,—
'Twas hard to call him but a brute, he knew
and felt so much.

We wandered then down to the brook beyond
    our sugar-place,
Where often at the old mill-hole I'd stood and
    bobbed for dace,
And once a big trout took my bait—I quiver-
    ed with delight—
Until my line caught on a snag quite hidden
    from my sight.

Throughout that Summer, day by day, at
    dawn, at noon, at eve,
I vainly angled for that trout more hours than
    you'd believe;
But while he thus outwitted me, I learned
    from Nature's book,
That boys can never be true boys unless they
    haunt some brook.

I woke to find these vanished scenes of child-
      hood's cherished hours

A dream of what they once had been, and only
      perished flowers;

Yet glad and grateful e'en for this, I search
      through memory's path

And pluck with joy each perfumed leaf from
      Dreamland's aftermath.

THY tender, thoughtful, earnest eyes—
Within their tranquil depths there lies
A magic power, unknown to thee,
That chains me in captivity.

The morning light the brighter grows
Wherever their effulgence glows,
And e'en at night their potent ray
Converts the darkness into day.

So would my pathway through each year
Of life's contending hope and fear,
Be made one blissful, hallowed spell,
Should such supernal light there dwell.

THE VOICE OF THE ROSE.

NCE happy I, when lone I dwelt,
   And ne'er a stranger's hand
   I felt, —
The hedge-row, lane and upland mine,
   Companioned with the herds and kine.

I then knew well each sister's face,
   Her gentle smile and growing grace,
While blooming there through summers long
   With honied bees and birds of song.

But oft I've seen, with trembling fear,
  Some idle school-boy loitering near
To pluck me in my morning pride,
  When I my blushing face would hide.

Through days we've watched, and each in turn,
  For moving bush, or bending fern,
To warn against intrusions there,
  That we our humble lives might spare.

While thorns that guarded each frail flower,
  True to their trust, enforced their power,
Yet still some ruthless hand each day
  Would pluck and bear our best away,—

Away perchance to stifling air
  To pour reluctant fragrance there,
Unnoticed by the boisterous throng
  Whose wine provokes their maudlin song;—

Or where in shame and worse despair
  'Twere tangled in some harlot's hair,
And through the long and hideous night
  Would languish, fade and die affright;—

Or where Love's gentle voice is heard—
  Mute witness to each spoken word—
Where his impassioned vows reveal
  The rapture which young lovers feel;—

Or where it decks the trembling bride
  When kneeling at the altar-side;
Or to her pathway where 'twould lend
  A fragrant Springtime to the end.

Or where the broken-hearted prays
  When fade life's gorgeous sunset rays,
With speechless lips and reverent head
  Its incense there is gladly shed;—

And we an equal homage yield
  To those whose faults were not concealed;—
With joy we linger at the grave
  Which man condemned, but God forgave."

Thus spoke the lowly-hearted rose
   And told its pleasures and its woes;
So henceforth let man's friendly hand
   Guard well these wonders God hath planned,

And treat them as a sacred trust
   (For they ask not but what is just)
And spare them from pollution where
   Their gracious fragrance fills the air —

Since only in the heavenly thought
   Were such ethereal marvels wrought: —
Our souls, by sparing these frail things,
   Are lifted as by angel wings.

MOUNT BLANC.

 TERNAL Mount, whose brow serene
    Rests pillowed on the clouds,
    half-seen,
What longing thy abode inspires
    In human hearts — what vast desires!

'Tis not decreed that mortal clod
    Should dwell on earth and still with God,
But thou, reared from the lowly vale,
    Dost in supernal realms prevail.

And then, as if thou hadst a soul
Pervading its celestial goal,
Thou hast attained and wearest now,
A spotless mantle for thy brow.

And He who did a promise give
That man shall more than mortal live,
Renews that emblem day by day,
That it may never fade away.

Thus, hallowed Mount, from realms divine
Thy coronet shall ever shine —
A beacon, beaming far and wide,
For weary, wayward feet a guide!

Chamounix, Aug. 30th, 1873.

TO JUSTIN S. MORRILL.

(A Senator of the United States from 1867 to 1899.)

ON HIS EIGHTY-THIRD BIRTHDAY,
APRIL 14TH, 1893.

IKE some o'ertowering forest oak that still
    Withstands the winds of four-score years
    and more,
While growths of younger years uprooted
    fall, —
Hoary with ripened leaf, but tried and strong

Thou standest waiting for those rapturous
   days
   When blooming fields, kissed by the vernal
   sun,
With fragrant breath speak gratitude.
   We hail thee now with fonder, firmer grasp,
Thankful to Him who rules all destines,
   That, well-nigh shivered by the furious blast [1]
Which bent thee low and made all hearts
   despair,
   Thou'rt left the stronger by the gale, and still
Can with thy friends rejoice this natal day
   To stand on earth though gazing into heaven!

And yet for worth and fame and all that makes
   Life grand and great, thou surely hast no
   need
To further go. Within the wondrous time
   Wherein thou led'st the panting legions on,

· [1] **A** serious illness.

The fettered have been freed, and hushed the
     sounds
Of curséd war whose awful uproar once
Convulsed the troubled land from sea to sea.
     Saved is the State, and hostile cannon now
Are molded into pryamids of peace!

The eager throngs that crowd our shores to join
     The Nation's jubilee,² may marvel much
Before the temple thou hast helped to rear
     To law and justice long denied, and mark
The mighty march of an enfranchised race
     Toward the blood-bought rights of men.

                         Old friend,
Thy well-earned rest has come. A grateful State
     Whose every cause was served so long, so well,
Withholds no added honor from thy name,
     But prays that thou shalt have forevermore
The crowning peace thou hast for others won!

     2 World's Columbian Exposition in 1893.

THE SERENADE.

HE smiling stars shine o'er my head,
For now the longing day hath fled
Whose hours seemed more than
years to me
Because they held me far from thee,—

From thee my sweet, my precious rose,
　　Now lost in dreams and soft repose —
In dreams of some far world of bliss,
　　For thou wert made too pure for this.

An Ariel would I gladly be,
　　And were I one I'd bear to thee
The choicest flowers that bud and bloom
　　To shed round thee their rare perfume.

I'd lure birds from their chosen climes
　　To sing for thee their sweetest rhymes,
For thy rare beauty would inspire
　　Their raptured souls with such desire.

O wake and listen to my song—
    That which hath pressed my heart so long—
And thus assuage its throbbing pain
    Though passion's fire shall still remain!

But if thy slumbers thou shalt keep,
    Of me I crave one thought may creep
Into thy visions, pure and blest,
    And then content this heart can rest.

CLARK AND THE OREGON.

HE Oregon at anchor lay, within the
Golden Gate,
And far remote from surging
waves — a thing inanimate —
When came an order, urgent, brief, to make
for Callao,
And there await — for war might be — and with
no dastard foe.
"All hands to anchor!" shouted Clark; then
tugged each groaning chain,
And, ere the night, that battleship was plough-
ing through the main.

And from that grave and anxious hour, for tid-
    ings still to learn,

She rushing, left her foaming wake, for lengths
    and lengths astern;

Along Pacific's coast she sped, as ship ne'er
    sped before,

Led by the Southern Cross whose beam each
    wave in sequence bore.

Callao reached, late orders read, at once for
    Rio sail,—

Then on she swept, like mountain mist, before
    a raging gale.

She leapt into Magellan's jaws—more dreaded
    than armed foes—

And safe beyond their reefs and rocks, wild
    cheer on cheer arose.

What though Cervera's fleet were met? — what
    though in wait it lay? —
Such danger made her falter not, but eager for
    the fray. —
What though her sailors hungry went, and
    knew not sleep, nor rest,
If, yielding what they needed most would serve
    their country best?
The sturdy stokers, nigh outworn, still hotter
    made the fires,
And not a man, though parched with thirst,
    once stopped to quench desires.
The North Star struggled from afar to throw
    its potent ray —
That beacon which the brightest burns when
    lighting Freedom's way.

Toward its beam, through wind and wave, the
battleship swept on,
While Clark stood constant on the bridge and
watched for lurking Don.
At length, she entered Rio's port, where late
dispatches bore
News that the dogs of war were loosed and
bayed along our shore.—
Then like a meteor she swept on to join our
fleet away
At Santiago's armored gate, where it held Spain
at bay.
The engineers, unconscious grown, by stifling
air, alack,
When borne to deck and half restored, tried
hard to stagger back;

And though this sovereign of the sea five thou-
    sand leagues had run,
This paragon of battleships, as fresh as when
    begun, —
With Clark at helm — with crew elate, — (this
    more than welcome guest) —
Unhalting, pushed to Sampson's line, then
    proved herself his best.

That Sabbath morn had calmly dawned, and
    through the languid air
Came far, faint sounds of convent bells that
    called to grateful prayer;
But Oh! what crashing thunders break when
    now the foemen meet! —
For look you there, — on swiftly comes Cer-
    vera's royal fleet —

Defiant, and with war-like mien, out through
the narrow bay!
All-desperate, they open fire and force the
awful fray,
But Sampson's roaring guns reply, "You're wel-
come here, come on!"—
And furies of a thousand hells are gathered
here in one!
Through ·smoke and fume the battle waged,
and every shell we sent
Was planted where it counted most, and where
our gunners meant:—
Then, leading all, the Oregon leapt foremost
to the van,
And raked .and riddled with her shells, each
deck that bore a man,—

While Clark forgot his conning-tower, where danger was the least,
And on his forward turret stood, where danger never ceased.
The Spainards read their tragic fate in their doomed cruisers' light,
And all aflame, dashed on the shore, and thus gave up the fight.

Henceforth, on fame's eternal page, the Oregon will shine,
And Clark—that brave "Green-Mountain Boy"—will be in every line,—
That hill-born hero of the waves, whose name revered will be,
So long as valor has a place in annals of the sea.

Elsewhere they vaunt their pedigrees, and boast
  of "royal blood,"
But through *his* veins coursed "royal blood"
  not made by man, but God—
The kind that captured old "Fort Ti.," and
  won at Bennington,
Where grand old Stark the Hessians fought,
  until the sinking sun.
While Clark and Dewey tread our decks—
  those peerless of our brave,—
From every mast, on every breeze, "Old
  Glory" still shall wave!

A MEMORY.

LOOKED upon such wondrous face,
  Such beauty, such surpassing
  grace,
Had ever artist once portrayed
  The faultless features I surveyed,
He would thereby have won a name
  Still absent from the page of fame.

While thus I gazed, intent, beguiled,
  The vision moved, and then it smiled,
And o'er a harp flew two white hands
  Like mated swallows o'er the sands.
Methought, what wondrous magic brings
  Such melting strains from those mute strings.—

Then Nature—not content to spare
  One gift or grace from her so fair—
She sang. Such sweet and tender notes
  Could only come from angel throats;—
A praising saint could not compare
  With sounds so touching and so rare.—

First came the warble ofı a bird; —
　Then but a human voice was heard; —
Then some yet more impassioned strain
　Infused my pulse and thrilled my brain.
As o'er the strand the billows roll,
　This lapped and laved my raptured soul.

But vain, indeed, it were to ask
　Ofı artist hand — unequal task —
To portray halfı the gifts divine
　Embodied there in every line, —
For, had one sought by art to trace
　The beauty ofı that matchless face,
The vision would have dazed the brain,
　And moveless must that hand have lain.

THE TESTY DEACON.

WAS down in the old Pine Tree
state
Where chanced to pass what I
relate,—
The land where pies and cakes abound,
And Yankees at their best are found;

Where natives serve their pork and beans
In methods fit for kings and queens,
And where French gastronomic art
Is not in vogue in any part.

'Twas in a rural farming town
  (That never yet had won renown)
Where dwelt a farmer — Ephraim Hale —
  The subject of this woful tale.

Now "Deacon Eph" as he was called
  Wore well his years, though long since bald,
And seemed to lead a righteous life
  Though mighty testy with his wife.

Long deacon in the village church
  His goodly name had known no smirch;
His neighbors all were proud that he
  Should such a model neighbor be.

Now one grave fault the deacon had
　　Which was a temper, always bad;
And this he lashed with passion's whip
　　And made it sting at every clip.

With Yankee thrift he money made
　　By keeping geese that often strayed
Unto his neighbor's very door
　　And wrecked his garden o'er and o'er.

One day this neighbor — Moses Slade —
　　Espied them, while in ambush laid —
Each delving like a lusty Turk
　　To ruin all his careful work.

He straightway ran and seized each goose
 And e're he turned the creature loose
Slit through the web between its toes
 And made *one* foot just like a crow's.

In panic then they hustled all
 To get beyond the garden wall,
And chose the shortest route for home
 Without desire to further roam.

They sought at once (by instinct led)
 The near-by pond where they were bred,
And then proceeded, one by one,
 To navigate as they had done.

But lo! their calculations failed,
　　And all acquatic ardor quailed
When round and round their bodies spun,
　　With not an inch ofi headway won.

When thus the deacon found his geese,
　　His rage foretold a breach ofi peace; —
He swore revenge on neighbor Slade
　　Though he through blood should have
　　　　to wade.

So, well disguised, the first dark night,
　　He sought his neighbor's barn for spite,
And seized the tail ofi his old mare
　　And sheared it clean ofi every hair.

Then farmer Slade was wroth in turn,
  And for revenge his heart did burn;—
He swore he'd "pickle old Hale's hide,
  And drive him from the church beside."

He sought a Justice of the Peace,
  And, (keeping mum about the geese,)
In his complaint discreetly swore
  Of what occurred the night before.—

Therein he charged one Ephraim Hale,
  In legal terms—full of detail—
With mutilating his old mare
  By shaving off her caudal hair.—

He further swore that the offense
　　Arose from malice, called " prepense,"
And that such act did violate
　　The peace and dignity ofi State.

He prayed the Justice there to grant
　　A warrant for the miscreant,
Which then was signed, with formal care,
　　And with a grave, judicial air.

'Twas with much craft that farmer Slade
　　On Saturday his charge had made,
So that arrest should fall that night
　　And thus make worse the deacon's plight.

Just at the hour of evening prayers
    Went forth the sheriff unawares
To make arrest of deacon Hale
    And take him to the county jail.

The deacon answered his loud knock
    As struck the hour of nine o'clock
And warmly bade him enter in
    As if he were his fondest kin.

The sheriff soon his mission told
    And then the warrant did unfold
Which he read through in solemn tones
    Oft punctured by the deacon's groans.

Then Ephraim, who was much enraged,
　　Tore like a tiger first encaged,
And charged upon that viper, Slade,
　　The outrage oft this foul crusade.

Though "Mother Hale" for mercy plead,
　　And grievous tears in plenty shed, —
All proved to be of no avail
　　To save her raving spouse from jail.

Full half that wretched night was o'er,
　　When swung the jailor's ponderous door
Through which the sheriff quickly passed
　　Together with his charge, held fast.

The deacon still with anger burned,
  Yet meekly to the jailor turned,
As if his mild and tender eye
  Betokened welcome sympathy.

"Tell me," said he, "what can I do
  To make my hours here brief and few?"—
"Until you're tried, you must get bail,"
  The jailor said, "or stay in jail."

"That will I do," quoth Hale, "this night,
  And leave this den before day-light,
Then to my church I'll promptly go
  And no one of this plight shall know."

"You can't do that," the jailor said,
 " For Justice lies asleep in bed; —
Besides, the Sabbath's now well on
 And that, in law, is *dies non.*"

The deacon never closed his eyes,
 But all that night tried to devise
The means whereby he might get bail
 And flee far from that curséd jail.

That Sabbath day he gave to prayer,
 And thoughts of sacred things elsewhere; —
His waiting home; his weeping wife,
 And church he'd missed not once through
  life.

When bail, at length, had been obtained
   And Ephraim had his freedom gained,
His homeward journey he began —
   A wiser, though much sadder man.

But he, alas, in church and out,
   Had enemies who had no doubt
That there was ample evidence
   To fix on him that grave offense.

A special meeting of the church
   Was called to instigate a search,
And a committee chosen there
   Was sent to view the hapless mare.

They found, indeed, the ancient brute
   Bereft of caudal growth hirsute,
But not one fact to prove, withal,
   Who plied the art tonsorial.

And so, their mission having failed,
   (A fact that most of them bewailed,)
There seemed to be no earthly clue
   Which they with hope could then pursue.

But, while in vain they tried, each one,
   To learn by whom the deed was done,
A tramp came sliding down the mow,
   Who told by whom, and when and how.—

He stated that on one dark night
　　While in the barn, appeared a light,
And that he "watched and saw old Hale
　　With sheep-shears trim that hosses tail."

"He knew" he said, "that old cuss well,"
　　And instances he then did tell,
When from his watch-dogged house he'd fled
　　While foraging for needful bread.

From what they thus had seen and heard
　　Their pious souls were deeply stirred,
And all agreed, with prompt accord,
　　To put the guilty to the sword, —

For now the church was up in arms,
    And for just once omitted psalms; —
Their model was in deep disgrace
    And in the church should have no place.

From office he was then deposed;
    His name was dropped; his pew was closed,
And neighbor Slade, who owned the mare,
    Was chosen deacon then and there.

The lesson of this touching tale,
    While dearly bought by Ephraim Hale,
Shows well how a few brainless geese
    A deacon taught to keep the peace!

COLUMBIA.

GODDESS, stay thy threatening hand
From alien hosts in that far land
Whose voice now rends the pity-
    ing sky
With plaintive cries for liberty!

The girdle 'neath thy throbbing breast
  Was forged from chains of those oppressed;
The stripes upon thy stola — these
  Are blood-stains of thy votaries.

The spangled cap that crowns thy head
  Was placed there by the martyred dead,
Who braved and bled and died in vain,
  If struggling Freedom shall not gain.

O, stretch thy helping arm to free
  The prostrate forms that kneel to thee,
And give to men, unjustly blamed,
  The sacred rights thy birth proclaimed!

January, 1899.

I THINK OF THEE.

THINK of thee when, dim and gray,
　　Belated, drowsy night is roused,
　　And loath to go, half-clad and slow,
Recedes before advancing day.

I think of thee when anxious care
　　Enslaves me through each labored hour;
But toil were sweet, with joy replete,
　　Could I for thee my burdens bear.

I think of thee with fonder heart,
  When day, commingling with the night,
Prolongs his kiss of transient bliss
  Like lovers when enforced to part.

Then in my hours of deep repose
  On thee my craving dreams still feast,
Yet when I wake, with hunger's ache,
  My yearning but intenser grows.

And thus my aching heart for thee
  Throbs on throughout each longing day, —
In wild desire, a quenchless fire,
  Till smothered by eternity.

THE WOODS.

FAIN to the vaulted woods I go, where
    solitude doth reign,
    And seat me on some lichened rock,
  a brief surcease to gain
From tumult of the maddening mart, where
    men contend for gold,
And barter governs every thought, though lives
    be bought and sold.—

Here would I breathe the balsamed air, the
freshness of the trees,
And listen to the song of birds, and hum of
gathering bees;
Ah, here is peace, supernal peace, a paradise
regained,
Where man can soothe his troubled soul and
feel himself enchained!

Here spread the hemlocks' feathery wings; here
lift the stately pines;
Here, whitened birches whiter seem, by ruddy,
clinging vines;
Here, too, the fruitful chestnuts tower, and in
the lengthening year,
With bursting burrs and shining nuts the
scampering squirrels cheer.

On yonder spruce, now spectral grown, and
aged with countless ills,
The lone woodpecker urgent raps, then listens
where he drills
To hear the toiling insect stir, where strips of
bark yet cling,
Then pecks again till one is found, and flies
on fleeter wing.

But hark! I hear the partridge drum, to call
his absent mate;
And then the silver-throated thrush his ecstacies
relate;
The veeries and the vireos make all the woods
rejoice,
And rapture comes when whip-poor-wills add
their enchanting voice.

God made no earthly place like this, to lull
    sad weary souls,
Where Nature's untrained orchestra beguiles and
    then consoles;
And as I tread the beaten path, down life's de-
    cending hill,
The transports of this sylvan spot will haunt
    and cheer me still!

VERMONT.

———

HY very name doth symbolize
    Thy verdant peaks that proudly
    rise,
As ift to buttress with their might
    The unpropped dome of heavenly light.

The beauty ofi thy matchless hills
　The ravished eye with rapture fills,
While thy fair fields and fertile plains
　Bear flocks and herds and bounteous grains.

Thy Druid forests still conceal
　The eagles that high o'er them wheel,
And shelter well the panting deer
　When driven from the open near.

Thy hillside homes and hamlets all
　Proclaim content and thrift withal;—
No servile lines yet mark the face
　Ofi thy courageous, sturdy race.

Such land is thine, sons of thy birth,
   Whose sires, with blood, paid Freedom's
      worth;
Who vanquished each invading foe
   And swept him back, or laid him low.

No trembling slave yet breathed thy air
   Whose shackles longer bound him there,
For, by thy ancient Bill of Rights [1]
   All men stood equal on thy heights.

O happy land, thus early blessed,
   Where all were free and none oppressed,
Thank well those sires whose master hand
   Built from thy rock and not thy sand!

[1] Vermont was the first of the States to prohibit Slavery by
Constitutional Convention, viz., July, 1777.

THE RETURN.

ROM childhood's village, years away,
    I once more trod its lonely street,
The morning of a summer's day,
Nor saw one face to know and greet.

I crossed the bridge where once the stream
   Ran dark and deep and hurriedly,
But now I saw — how like a dream —
   Its waters ripple languidly.

I saw, near by, the school-house, where
   In torments of captivity,
Full many a day, imprisoned there,
   Was to me an eternity.

But where my school-mates, at their task,
   Were daily gathered, halfı the year,
Desertion stared and seemed to ask:—
   "What stranger is now sauntering here?"

Hard by, the "meeting-house" still stood
  Where, in my boyhood, old and young
Met in one common brotherhood
  To worship God with reverent tongue.

How memory now brought in review
  My childhood friends once gathered there;
The gray, now gone; the young I knew,
  Themselves now gray with years and care.

Methought, alas, how many score
  Had, in their last majestic state,
Been brought from out its ample door
  To pass, since then, yon church-yard gate.

I entered there among the dead;
  Then slowly strolled past chiseled stones,
And here, anon, I paused and read
  The fond names of remembered ones.

Such caravan of years had passed
  Since I this grass-grown path had trod,—
'Twas now a marbled city vast,
  Of those whose souls repose with God.

With heavy heart, I wandered on
  Through neighboring aisles still narrower,
Until, at last, I came upon
  The hallowed spot where kindred were.

And standing, with its lines severe,
   Their marble monolith I viewed,—
Pure as an angel's frozen tear,—
   Fit emblem oft their lives renewed.

But Nature comforts my sad heart,—
   For her enduring smiles here rest,—
Where buds and blossoms fain impart
   A fragrance that seems hallowed, blest;

Where suns first kiss the breast oft Spring,
   And birds are lured from chosen ways,
And, resting here their weary wing,
   Outpour their sweetest roundelays;—

Where blossoms hid amongst the bowers
   Are sought by humming birds and bees,
Who bring their sweets from distant flowers
   To dwell enraptured here with these.

And as o'er tides I'm swept along
   To wakeless dreams on sightless shore,
My benediction would prolong
   Peace to their dust, forevermore!

THE ALCHEMIST.

THAT peerless Alchemist, the heart,
   Transcending the magician's art,
   Imbues each tear, by passion
    wrought,
With distillations ofι our thought.

And hence emotion's laden tear
   Knows more than wisest sage or seer
Or oceans vast, that ebb and flow,
   Ofι human joy and human woe.

CHILDHOOD'S DREAM.

H, blesséd was that childhood day,
When with sweet Alice, blithe
and gay,
I tripped adown the country lane,
Her hand in mine — her gallant swain.

O, she was more than Saxon fair
   With sunbeams nestled in her hair,
While from her gladsome, heaven-blue eyes
   One caught the gleams of paradise.

Her lips were like two rubies set
   With pearls between — I see them yet —
As when she, blushing, to me said,
   "I love you, if you love me, Ned."

I answered in no doubting way,
   Down in the lane that joyful day;
And thence our two hearts beat as one
   And few were hours they beat alone.

No darkening shadow, cloud or mist
   Pervaded that secluded tryst,
But every sun shone full and fair
   And taught its rays to linger there.

Life then was one sweet reverie;
   Its rhythm one fond melody;
That melody one gentle voice
   Whose accents bade my heart rejoice.

But lo! what grief soon pierced my heart
   And sent its pang to every part
When illness came, and Alice died,
   And wondering angels turned and sighed.

And since that day, how vainly I
　　Have tried to solve life's mystery, —
To understand why buds that bloom
　　Should, ere their fruitage, reach their
　　　　doom ; —

Why childhood, fresh and fair and pure
　　Should be the one for death to lure,
While age is left to totter through
　　Still other years, concealed from view.

Life's noon had passed, ere once again
　　I wandered through that hallowed lane,
And lo, how changed! — few signs it bore
　　That I had trod its path before.

I sought that humble cottage near,
  Which through my childhood was so dear,
But found it not; where once it stood
  Were tangled weeds and blackened wood.

With saddened heart I turned to go,
  But spied, hard by, a headstone low,
Whereat I paused, and through my tears,
  Read — "Here lies Alice: aged ten years."

THE AWAKENING.

T length the mystic touch of Spring
   Awakes the slumbering forms of
   earth,
When Nature spreads her warming wing,
And blesses all with glad rebirth.

Her breath infuses every breeze
   With odors and perfumes divine,
Drawn from the blossomed apple trees
   And every fragrant bud and vine.

Now robins sing their sweetest song —
   And bobolinks and orioles, —
Sweetest because suppressed so long
   It bursts from out their brimming souls.

Now comes the chirp of building birds;
   The noisy caw of watchful crows;
While from the hill-side's browsing herds
   The distant cow-bell's tinkle flows.

The blackbirds from the willows cry;
   The plover pipes in yonder bogs,
And from the stagnant pool, hard by,
   Rise amorous murmurings of the frogs.

Such mingled sweets and rhapsodies
   Soothe every sense with anodynes; —
In vain I strive, through languor's eyes,
   To comprehend God's vast designs!

THE night was starless, bleak and
drear,
And through the rigging one
could hear
The wild winds blowing, bearing moans
Discordant to the ear, and groans
Of ship, now tossed from side to side,
As on she trembled o'er the tide.

Yet plunged she through the stormy way,
  With throes that brought but pale dismay
To stalwart hearts, appalled by fear,
  That sent to cheeks the anxious tear
Lest kindred on a distant shore,
  Might wait, alas, forevermore.

Beneath the deck's low, creaking beam,
  In calm repose and joyful dream,
An aged mother, lone and ill,
  Throughout the tempest slumbered still,
Whose lamp of life, with fading ray,
  Foretold her near and final day.

Long widowed, she had lived through toil
  On distant Scotland's storied soil;
For, one by one, at man's estate,
  Their pulses strong, their hearts elate,
Her sons had sought far western shores
  Where Plenty stood at opened doors.

And thus, with all life's sunshine lost,
  Time touched her with its wilting frost;
Then years grew long, and dark the way,
  Like shadows at departing day,
And fondest of her dreams were fain
  To clasp and kiss her boys again.

Through night and storm and troubled sea
   She slumbered on in ecstacy,
Still dreaming of her darling boys
   And future years of waiting joys;—
But ere the cloud-swept sun arose
   Her soul had fled from all its woes.

That morn so bright, in steerage lay—
   Its spirit fled—the mortal clay;
And soon the sailors' heavy tread
   Bore to the deck the humble dead,
In canvas shroud, with cordage bound,
   While wailing sea-gulls hovered round.

Then near the dead and yet along,
　　There huddled sailors, mute and strong,
Who lowered down the vessel's side
　　That muffled form to waters wide,
Which sank beneath the wave's embrace,
　　Whose sepulchre no kin can trace.

For her no tolling bell was heard,
　　Nor sob, nor sigh, nor spoken word;
But memories yet will toll a knell
　　In hearts that still remember well
Their slumbers soft, and blissful rest,
　　Upon that mother's loving breast.

UNDAUNTED.

AY, lingering at the western door,
    Looks back, with taper in his
    hand,
And dimly lights the purple floor,
    Whereon approaching Night will stand.

Throughout the heaven's boundless height
  Hang twilight's lamps now burning low,
But as they spy the goddess, Night,
  They greet her with their brightest glow.

She, stealing from her hidden bowers —
  Her faithful service to maintain —
Patrols the dark and lonely hours,
  To guard, in turn, Day's vast domain.

Together, they, like sentinels,
  Have paced through centuries that were,
Which, huddled in their mouldy cells,
  Repose in Time's vast sepulchre.

Since parting at primeval dawn —
   When last he saw her beauteous face —
Day has pursued this nimble fawn
   With yearning heart and eager pace.

Unwearied by his futile chase;
   Undaunted, too, by cruel fate,
Yet yearning for one fond embrace,
   Each morn he bursts the Orient gate.

His passion now resistless grown,
   He throws his arms from roseate bowers;
But timid Night, alert, has flown,
   And left her tears upon the flowers.

ACROSS THE STREET.

———

o club-house "swells" who crowd,

   en masse,

To stare at maidens as they

   pass, —

On that vain throng, just out of bed,

   Which turns its eyes, but not its head, —

For adoration decked, arrayed,

   In "stunning" clothes, all "ready-made;" —

A scene like this, to dudish eyes,

   Is like a glimpse of paradise.

But now and then a clubless man
    May have his day Elysian,
For, as he homeward plods at night,
    There may from off the car alight
(Just at the corner where he dwells)
    Some Aphrodite who excels
The Grecian goddess in the grace
    And beauty of her classic face: —
And then, (since luck has turned his way,)
    May learn, perchance, the following day
That this rare maid lives in the *suite*
    That faces his, across the street; —
A creature far more shy than bold;
    With glowing cheeks and hair of gold;
Whose eyes have stole the skies' own blue;
    Whose lips would pale the poppy's hue;
Whose form so luscious, ripe and rare,
    'Twould seem to charm the very air
Through which she moves, with faultless grace,
    To hide, at times, her roguish face. —

Yes, once I met a celibate
    Who vouched for what I thus relate.
He proved to be that very man—
    (The one without a club or clan,)
Who then proceeded to narrate
    The outcome of his harrowing fate:—

"From out my window, hour by hour,
    I once watched Nature's fairest flower.
She smiled in most bewitching ways,
    And each month flirted thirty days
Most ardently, yet so reserved,
    That had bread been thus scantly served,
I starved each day while lingering yet
    To gaze upon this rare coquette."

"So while this maid, in that coy way,
    Thus tortured me from day to day,
I realized how very fine
    Grandmother Prude had drawn the line

Permitting, say, a hundred smiles,
  But kept us dumb as two gargoyles."

"But science, ah, that brought relief,
  Just when I might have come to grief.
I therefore bought a telephone —
  Which lovers' service oft had done —
(Since Madame Grundy's stern decree
  O'erlooked this form of ecstacy,)
Then drank the nectar, sip by sip,
  In accents from her honied lip,
Until my brain took wings and flew
  To realms whereof it never knew,
Where sweet communion was ordained
  And more than former joys attained,
'Till, Icarous-like, the heated wires
  Were melted by our ardent fires;
And when, in haste and unawares,
  I dropped to earth to make repairs,
This charmer stood, at her front door,
  Coquetting with my janitor!"

TO MARJORIE.

(A DÉBUTANTE)

———

MARJORIE, with brow so fair, and
    heart so chaste and pure,
    The world adoring thee beholds
    thy fit investiture;
,For now, in queenly robes thou standst, a bride
    to coming years,
As smiling Future beckons thee, while stands
    the Past in tears.
O goddess of the present, thou! O vision of
    the morrow!
Thy younger comrades bid adieu with heavy
    heart and sorrow.

L. of C.

May every fond, enchanting dream of childhood's happy hour,

Bring forth its glad reality, and every bud its flower.

But as life's pathway thou dost tread, and up its steeps dost climb,

Choose for thy comrades Charity, and Hope and Faith sublime; —

Then thou hast taught humanity how justly thou hast earned,

The heavenly radiance from above, that on thy head is turned.

THE PRODIGAL.

HY should man loiter by the way—
　　A vagrant through each golden
　　day?
And why should he so weary grow
　　With countless blessings here below?
And why complain that he should share
　　Such burdens as his fellows bear,
And live but for life's joys alone,
　　Nor grateful be, for every one?

The mighty oak's concentric ring
   Counts well each oft-recurring Spring;—
The sands when dropping from the glass
   Hold back the seconds as they pass;—
The time-worn clock in yonder tower
   Reluctant tolls each passing hour,
And nought but man, by reckless haste,
   Permits one precious hour to waste,
Nor like a spendthrift, seeks to borrow
   For use to-day, hours of the morrow.
Will such a squanderer ever learn
   His lamp of life to wisely burn,
So that the oil shall feed its ray
   To light his feet at close of day!